THE ULTIMATE
WEDDING MUSIC KIT

Music, Planning Tips and more for the perfect wedding

Shawnee Press, Inc.
A Subsidiary of Music Sales Corporation
Nashville, TN 37212

Visit Shawnee Press Online at **www.shawneepress.com/songbooks**

Contents

A Musical Tour of Your Wedding

The Prelude / Pre-Ceremony

This is the very beginning of the wedding, the time when the first guests arrive; sometimes refreshments and hors d'oeuvres are served before the Ceremony begins. Listen to a few samples of music from the included CDs as you imagine the setting of your wedding and visualize your first guests arriving.

• Air on the G String	J. S. Bach
• Meditation	Jules Massenet
• Spring (from The Four Seasons)	Vivaldi

The Processional

The entrance of the Wedding Party for the Groom, and then for the Bride is considered the actual processional. Picture your family and friends, breathlessly waiting for the Processional to start, and then your wedding party walking down the aisle as you listen to Processionals on the CDs.

• Canon in D	Pachelbel
• Ave Verum Corpus	Mozart
• Jesu, Joy of Man's Desiring	J. S. Bach

The Bride's Entrance

This is the moment everyone's been waiting for... the moment the bride enters and walks down the aisle with her dad, parents or another significant person. Imagine yourself walking down the aisle as you listen to different choices ranging from dramatic to stately to more traditional.

• Bridal Chorus	Wagner
• Our Great Savior	Chapman / Prichard
• Trumpet Tune	H. Purcell

The Recessional

The joyous, post-Ceremony return down the aisle of you, your spouse, and your newly joined families is the conclusion of the ceremony and is directly followed by the guests' exit. Your music can be bright, joyful and upbeat.

• The Wedding March	Mendelssohn
• Trumpet Voluntary	J. Clarke
• Brandenburg Concerto No. 3 in G	J. S. Bach

NOTE: The musical selections from various categories can be somewhat interchangeable depending on personal tastes and individual needs.

Air On The G String

Composed by Johann Sebastian Bach

The Arrival Of The Queen Of Sheba

Composed by George Frideric Handel

8

The Water Is Wide

Traditional, Arranged by David Pearl

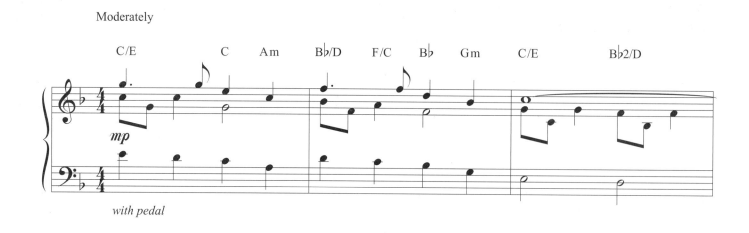

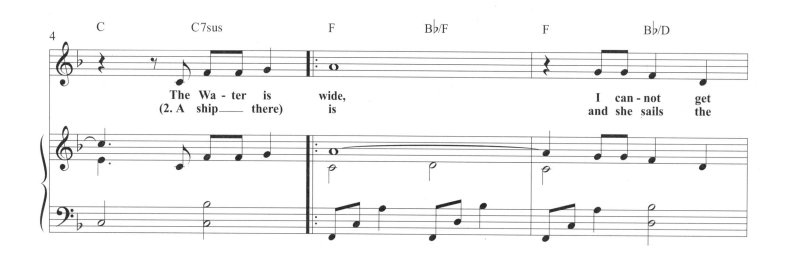

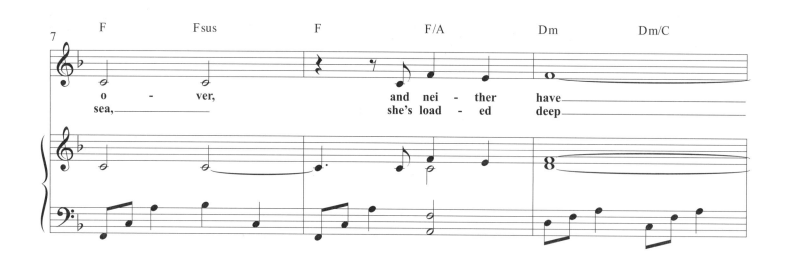

Our Great Savior

J. Wilbur Chapman; Rowland H. Prichard

Verse 1
> **Jesus! what a Friend for sinners!**
> **Jesus! Lover of my soul;**
> **Friends may fail me, foes assail me,**
> **He, my Savior, makes me whole.**

Refrain
> **Hallelujah! what a Savior!**
> **Hallelujah! what a Friend!**
> **Saving, helping, keeping, loving,**
> **He is with me to the end.**

Verse 2
> **Jesus! what a Strength in weakness!**
> **Let me hide myself in Him.**
> **Tempted, tried, and sometimes failing,**
> **He, my Strength, my vict'ry wins.**

Ave Verum Corpus, K618

Composed by Wolfgang Amadeus Mozart

Not too slow

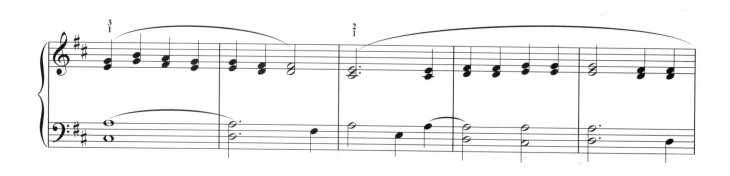

Brandenburg Concerto No. 3 in G
(First movement: Allegro)

Composed by Johann Sebastian Bach

Bridal March

Composed by Richard Wagner

23

Canon in D

Composed by Johann Pachelbel

27

29

Air
(from 'The Water Music')

Composed by George Frideric Handel

Double Violin Concerto
(Second movement: Largo)

Composed by Johann Sebastian Bach

Eine Kleine Nachtmusik, K525

(First movement: Allegro)

Composed by Wolfgang Amadeus Mozart

41

Für Elise

Composed by Ludwig Van Beethoven

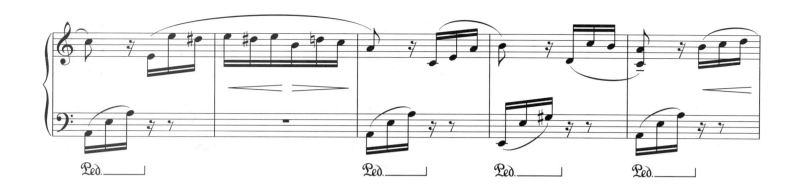

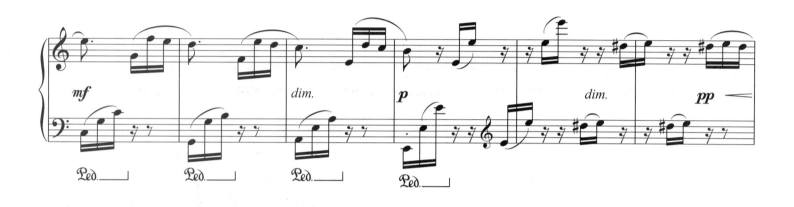

meno mosso

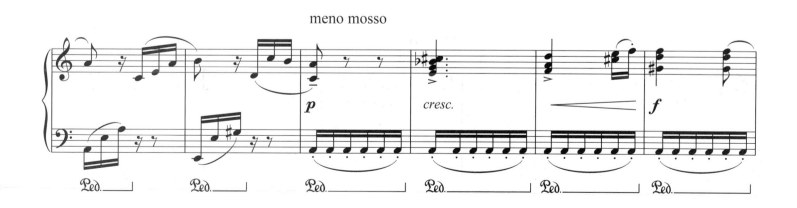

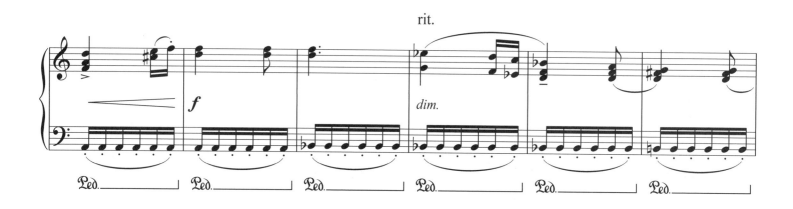

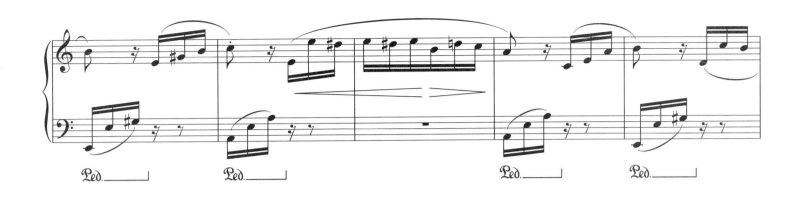

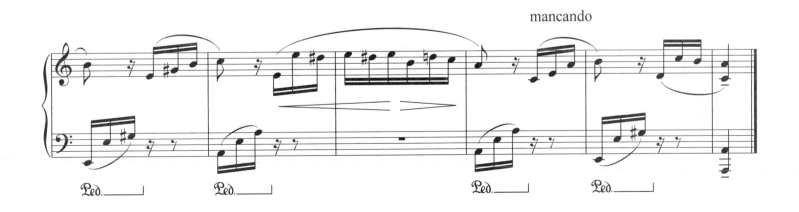

Gloria
(from 'Gloria')

Composed by Antonio Vivaldi

senza rall.

Grand March
(from 'Aida')

Composed by Giuseppe Verdi

Hallelujah Chorus
(from 'The Messiah')

Composed by George Frideric Handel

Hornpipe
(from 'The Water Music')

Composed by George Frideric Handel

Alla hornpipe

D.C. al Fine

Greensleeves

Traditional Irish Tune

Flowing and expressive, in one ♩. = 40 to 50

with pedal

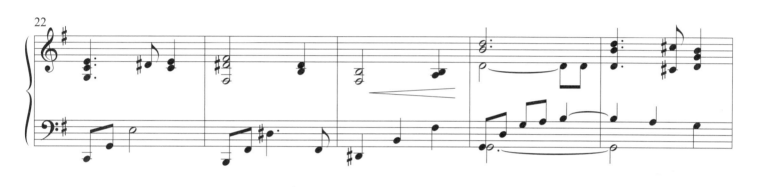

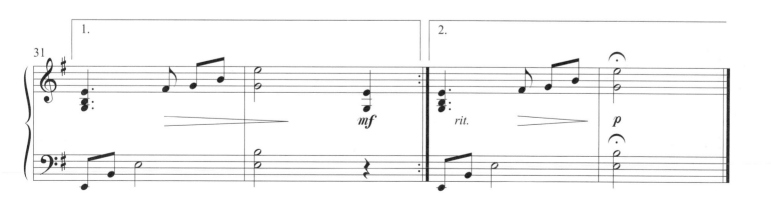

Be Thou My Vision

Ancient Irish Hymn, translated by Mary E. Byrne; Irish folk melody

Verse 3

Be Thou my battle Shield, Sword for the fight;
Be Thou my Dignity, Thou my Delight;
Thou my soul's Shelter, Thou my high Tower:
Raise Thou me heavenward, O Power of my power.

Verse 4

Riches I heed not, nor man's empty praise,
Thou mine inheritance, now and always:
Thou and Thou only, first in my heart,
High King of heaven, my Treasure Thou art.

Verse 5

High King of Heaven, my victory won,
May I reach heaven's joys, O bright heaven's Sun!
Heart of my own heart, whatever befall,
Still be my Vision, O Ruler of all.

Because

Edward Teschemacher/Guy d'Hardelot

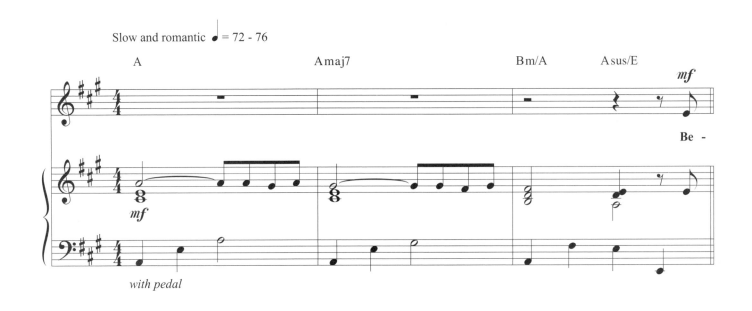

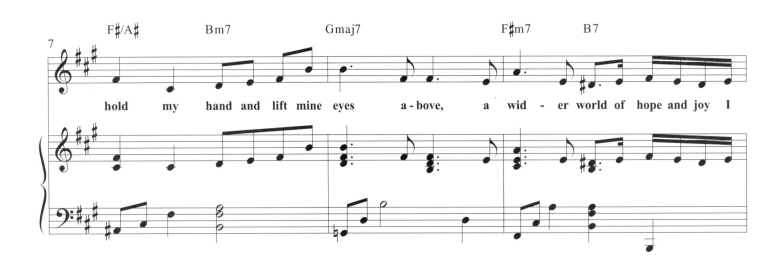

Joyful, Joyful, We Adore Thee

Henry van Dyke; Ludwig van Beethoven (melody from 9th Symphony)

With great joy! ♩ = 100 - 108

Verse 1

All Thy works with joy surround Thee,
Earth and heav'n reflect Thy rays,
Stars and angels sing around Thee,
Center of unbroken praise.

Field and forest, vale and mountain,
Flow'ry meadow, flashing sea,
Chanting bird and flowing fountain,
Call us to rejoice in Thee.

Verse 2

Thou art giving and forgiving,
Ever blessing, ever blest,
Wellspring of the joy of living,
Ocean depth of happy rest!

Thou our Father, Christ our brother—
All who live in love are Thine;
Teach us how to love each other,
Lift us to the joy divine.

Jesu, Joy of Man's Desiring

Words by Robert Bridges; Composed by Johann Sebastian Bach

Drawn by the
Where the

Thee, our souls as - pir - ing,
flock in Thee con - fid - ing,

Soar to un - cre - at - ed light.
Drink of joy from death - less springs.

Bist Du Bei Mir

(You Are With Me)

By Johann Sebastian Bach

Entreat Me Not to Leave Thee

(Song of Ruth)

Words and Music by Charles Gounod

(from the Book of Ruth 1:16-17)

where thou lodg - est, I will lodge._____ Thy

un poco meno presto, ma pochissimo

peo - ple shall be my peo - ple,

and thy_____ God, my God;_____ Thy

peo - ple shall be my peo - ple, and thy

God, _____ my God; _____ Thy

peo - ple shall be my peo - ple, and thy

God, my God.

Where thou di - est, will I die, _____ and

there will I be bur-ied;—— The Lord do so to me, and more

al - so, if aught but death part thee and me, if aught but

death—— part thee and me.—— Thy

peo - ple shall be my peo - ple,

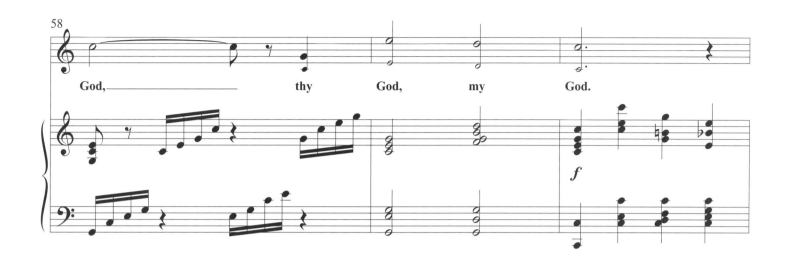

God,_____ thy God, my God.

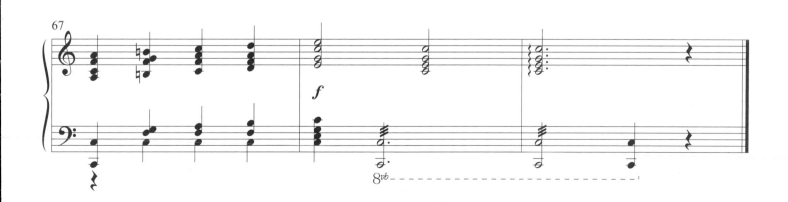

Meditation
(from 'Thaïs')

Composed by Jules Massenet

Minuet
(from 'String Quartet')

Composed by Luigi Boccherini

TRIO

O For The Wings Of A Dove

Composed by Felix Mendelssohn

Panis Angelicus
(O Lord Most Holy)

Composed by César Franck

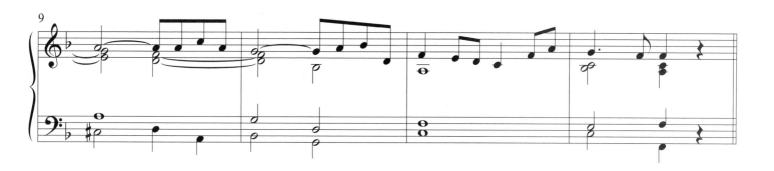

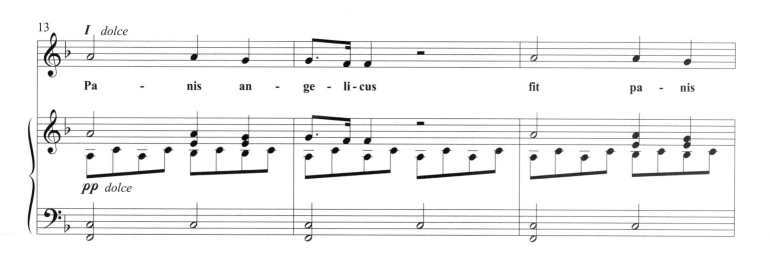

Pa — nis an — ge-li-cus   fit pa — nis

In Heavenly Love Abiding

Anna L. Waring; Felix Mendelssohn

Verse 3

Green pastures are before me, which yet I have not seen.
Bright skies will soon be over me, where darkest clouds have been.
My hope I cannot measure, my path to life is free.
My Savior has my treasure, and He will walk with me.

O the Deep, Deep Love of Jesus

Samuel Trevor Francis; Traditional Gaelic melody

Sheep May Safely Graze

Composed by Johann Sebastian Bach

D.C. al fine.

102

Oh, Promise Me!

Clement Scott; Reginald de Koven

Spring (from 'The Four Seasons')
(First movement: Allegro)

Composed by Antonio Vivaldi

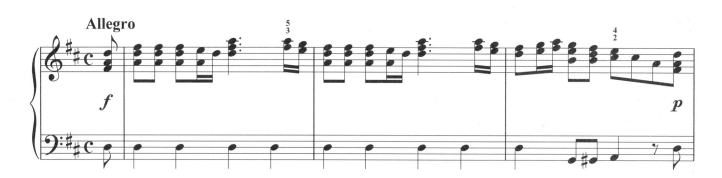

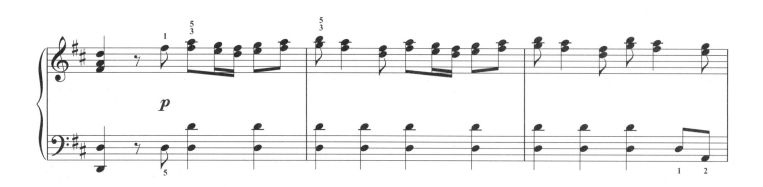

Trumpet Tune

Henry Purcell

Trumpet Tune

Henry Purcell

B♭ Trumpet Solo

Trumpet Voluntary

Composed by Jeremiah Clarke

Trumpet Voluntary

Composed by Jeremiah Clarke

B♭ Trumpet Solo

Jerusalem

W. Blake/H. Parry

I Love You Truly

Traditional

Sweetly, moderate tempo

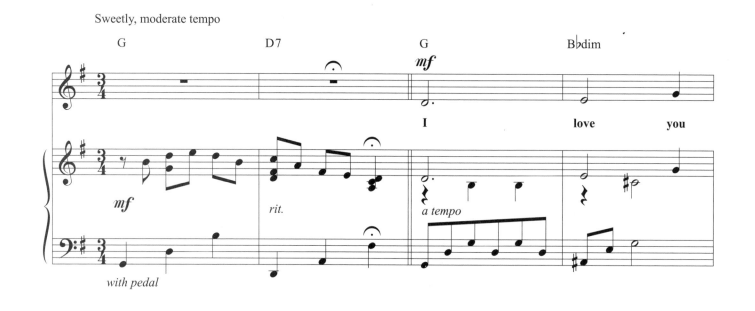

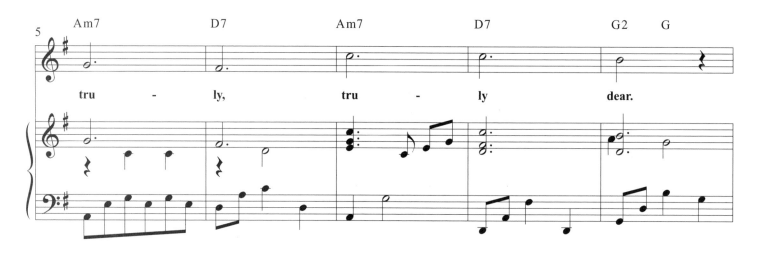

119

Wedding March
(from 'A Midsummer Night's Dream')

Composed by Felix Mendelssohn

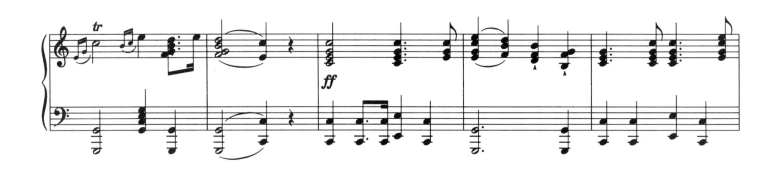

Prelude in A major Op. 28 No. 7

Composed by Frédéric Chopin

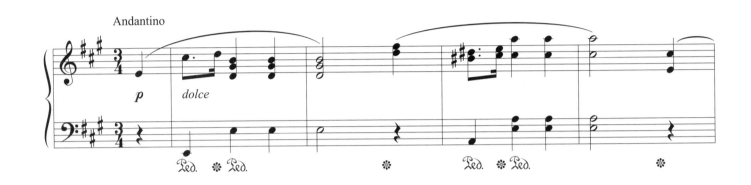

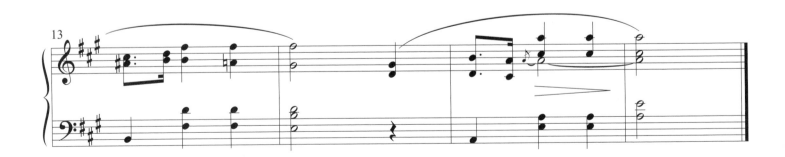

Other Special Moments

The Unity Candle

An optional but increasingly popular part of the Ceremony, the unity candle is a formal candle-lighting and brief period of prayer and reflection as you join your two lives (and your families) as one.

- Be Thou My Vision — Ancient Irish Hymn
- Meditation — Jules Massenet
- Jerusalem (Of English tradition) — Blake/Parry

The Interlude / Postlude

This is the time immediately after the wedding Ceremony and just before the main Reception. It's often the time set aside to be congratulated formally in a receiving line, or informally while pre-dinner beverages and hors d'oeuvres are being served. Sometimes it's used for picture-taking, especially when the bride and groom haven't seen each other before the ceremony out of custom or religious reasons.

- Für Elise — Beethoven
- Greensleeves — Trad. Irish tune
- Sheep May Safely Graze — J. S. Bach

The Reception

The time after the Ceremony is for celebrating--whether sit-down dinner, buffet or light refreshments-and it's always after the Interlude. (Not all weddings have interludes, or full dinner or dance receptions, but virtually all weddings have music.)

Most receptions start with a 'GRAND ENTRANCE' of the Bride and Groom usually accompanied by an up-beat piece of music. Sometimes, the whole wedding party is included. But this 'scene' of the wedding is usually one that's more important to brides and grooms.

- Eine Kleine Nachtmusik (1st mvmt.) — Mozart
- Gloria (from "Gloria") — Vivaldi
- Hornpipe (from The Water Music) — Handel
- Joyful, Joyful, We Adore Thee (9th Symph.) — Beethoven

First Dance, and Father / Daughter Dance

Every family has its own history and that can be reflected in the songs you choose for your dances. One of the best loved traditions is the Father/daughter dance. As you listen, to songs on the CDs, think of the different feelings you or your Father may want to express.

- Because — Teschemacher / G. d'Hardelot
- I Love You Truly — Carrie Jacobs-Bond
- Minuet (from String Quartet) — Boccherini
- O the Deep, Deep Love of Jesus — S. Francis/Gaelic melody
  (same melody as "Morning Has Broken")
- Oh, Promise Me! — C. Scott/R. de Koven

"Staging" the music for your wedding

Anyone can hire musicians for a wedding and put them up front to play, sing, etc. But by using some creative thinking and "staging" in the process, your wedding music can be not only creative but memorable for you and all who attend.

Whether you choose to have your wedding in a church, a hotel, a home or outdoors, you need to consider how and where your musicians are best physically placed. There are also certain things you can do to heighten the impact of the music presented based on how and where the musicians are placed.

1. Church wedding. This is the most frequent choice of where to have a wedding. Church sanctuaries come in different shapes and sizes, so if you're having your wedding in a sanctuary unfamiliar to you, you will need to carefully examine the space available for any musicians you use.

For example, if you are going to have a vocalist with piano and/or organ accompaniment, you might consider placing the vocalist in the balcony (if there is a balcony) while the organ or piano are probably located in the front of the sanctuary. The vocalist will probably need a microphone if placed in the balcony. You may want to put the vocalist in the foyer (or "Narthex" is it's called in some churches) for one song, then move that person to the front for the remainder of the ceremony.

Choir lofts often present challenges or opportunities for staging. If you're going to have a string quartet and the choir loft offers little room on the platform for an ensemble, you'll need to make sure there's enough room, or consider having the ensemble to the left or right of the area where the wedding party will be placed. Choir lofts can also offer different ways to have singers and/or instrumentalists placed in a visually interesting way. For example, if you have a vocal quartet and flutist (accompanied by piano and/or organ) you could have the vocalist on one level (row) in the choir loft while the instrumentalist(s) is on another level in the choir loft.

If you use a solo trumpet, flutist, cello, etc. with piano and/or organ, you might place the instrumentalist in the balcony or foyer (and then possibly move that person to the front for later in the ceremony for variety). Such movement can be done inconspicuously by having the instrumentalist exit from the front of the church (if beginning in the foyer) and then entering the front of the sanctuary (at the choir loft, for example) at a time during the ceremony when other movement is taking place.

2. Non-church wedding. All the above information regarding, instrumentalists, staging ideas, and so on apply to weddings held in homes, hotels, or other locations as well. You will need to make sure there are not other events at or near your chosen location which might complicate your event. For example, if you choose a hotel near a theme park, is there an event at that theme park on the day of your wedding which might complicate traffic? If you choose a hotel downtown in a city, is there ample parking for your guests? This is a "staging" consideration as well.

3. Outdoor wedding. The outdoors provides unlimited possibilities for staging. Use hills, ponds, trees, for key entrances and exits, music placement, etc. For example, consider having the family members (i.e., parents) enter from one area while the wedding party enters from another, and the bride yet another. Have the instrumentalist(s) placed strategically and creatively (around a pond or under a nearby tree, for example). Amplification becomes very important if using different placement areas, so consult a good sound technician.

For in depth wedding music planning, CDs and exclusive downloads visit:
www.weddingmusiccentral.com